Also by Anthony Sciarratta

Finding Forever: A 1970s Love Story

The Letter

FAITH IN
THE UNKNOWN

ANTHONY SCIARRATTA

A POST HILL PRESS BOOK
ISBN: 978-1-64293-443-4
ISBN (eBook): 978-1-64293-444-1

Faith in the Unknown
© 2020 by Anthony Sciarratta
All Rights Reserved

Cover art by Cody Corcoran

Post Hill Press
New York • Nashville
posthillpress.com

Published in the United States of America

For my oak tree, with deep roots in the soil of the earth.
We will always weather the storms that pass.

CONTENTS

FREE FLOWING WATER

With gleaming blue eyes
that shine like the color of the sea
you mold to life like water
flowing ever so freely.

Washing away my troubles with ease
as the tide flows up to my knees
feeling the chills flow down my spine
it was time to give in, the water was a sign.

So sensual and flowing, molding your body to mine
refreshing and warm tasting, sweet like red wine
pressing yourself against me in just about every way
cradling me as the wind blew across the bay.

Crashing around me, the water swept me away
taking me for a ride, there was peace in my mind for a day
the water molded the shape of my brain
washing away my troubles, ending their reign.

Water molds to anything, even my crazy mind
reminding me that you'll love me, until the end of time
you let me know I'm worth it and make me feel alive
giving me the courage to hope and to strive.

BLUE JAY AMONG THE BLACKBIRDS

My soul, innocent and fragile, like that of a bird
fractured by those who loved me
darkness is what they brought me
like blackbirds stalking their prey.

Amongst the acorns, soil, and twigs
the blackbirds squawk, one, two, and three
each saying different words
with meaning that hurts the soul of this bird.

A bright light between the blackbirds
this force, fierce in nature, not daring to waiver
delicate and beautiful to those staring
floating with the coming of a breeze.

With a soft white coat and snowy blue top
she was forever different from those around her
always daring to fly astray from the flock
the lonely Blue Jay waits.

She never wishes to fly alone
in a world that could be so bleak
attacked by the blackbirds one too many times
a mate for life is what she seeks.

She wants intelligence, first and foremost
judging the birds around her with swift thought
not easily impressed by what she sees
it was he who stood out, just like her.

Veering from the flock, side by side
they helped each other heal, leaving behind their pride
the blackbirds couldn't hurt them anymore
fearing only time, for when that ends, nobody is sure.

Together they will weather all the storms
standing true, never daring to break form
comfortable and cozy in a warm nest
the blackbirds, never to be seen again
not daring to put these two birds to the test.

FEAR

A tremble of fear runs through my heart
it's no paradox or mystery.
I fear losing a part of my soul
a woman only God could bring to me.

I fear sickness and death
no chance to say goodbye
happiness, taken in one stride
without mercy.

Powerless in a world of uncertainty,
as I try to control the world around me.
I'm only able to watch from where I am,
praying love will stand the test of time.

I want to be the force in your life,
the man you look to for comfort and love
filled with undying loyalty to you
and our God above.

Hoping to take the pain from your mind
and the sorrow from your heart.
Love is the only medicine
for those who suffer silently.

I sought asylum in your heart,
everlasting comfort in your body,
and passion in your mind.
I fear I'd lose all this, in a world that isn't kind.

A WRITER'S LIFE

I write with emotion,
feelings painful yet true.
The words bleeding onto the page
to tell the world of my struggle.

The pen is an escape
guided by those I love.
I create a fantasy I can control
filled with desperation to be remembered.

In my stories, you can live forever,
an immortal soul sealed in print,
a tale told over and over again
in one endless moment.

We have all felt how painful it is to be alive,
torn between the beauty of the world
and the terror of our minds.
I use my words as a guide
to capture a lifetime.

THE CHANGING TIDES

The tides change with the shape of the moon
like the chords in your mind change their tune.
I often wonder which woman I will get next
there are three I see, and all of
them leave me perplexed.

First there's my quirky girl, with
her head in the clouds,
the chatty, funny one who likes to sing aloud
a childlike personality filled with innocence,
she dances along to all the instruments.

Hiding deep inside is the lioness
with the mind of an evil scientist.
The half-moon witch, lurking beneath the kindness,
a mere look could render me lifeless.

The last is the most powerful of them all,
my dirty girl, the beautiful blonde that stands tall.
She's intelligent, cunning, and seductive,
yet not afraid to be instructive.

She's proud of her body, and the
curves that come along,
like the alluring seduction of a siren's song.
The way she looks at me with piercing eyes,
not willing to stop until she's satisfied.

As the tide continues to change in size,
she'll see how much I want her,
when I look into her eyes.
I'm only a man who feels so alone,
waiting for the next shape of the moon,
the greatest woman I've ever known.

1:55

Watching the clock tick away
counting as the moments go by
I wait for this time day by day
suddenly feeling spry.

My hands on the door, ready to leave
until I heard my phone beep
my eyes glazed over, I refused to believe
I sat in silence without a peep.

Thinking you were just fine
I tried to act as normal as could be.
I drove down the block for a sign
as if I were endlessly lost at sea.

Glass broke, and plastic smashed
you lay on the ground across the grass.
A blood-soaked shirt from a gash
sirens rang as an ambulance passed.

I sat at church in the third pew
after coming so close to losing you.
Because the truth is, you don't have a clue
how lost I would be without you.

A NIGHT OF DREAMS

As I fall asleep at night
I can't help but think of you.
I picture me, holding you tight
you look so beautiful from my view.

The feeling of your soft skin on mine
your body, taking my breath away
our blood, warm from the red wine
hoping the sun never comes up the next day.

I kissed your forehead, because I love your mind
peeling away the layers like a delicate flower.
Gently running my fingers down your spine
laying in a bed that we could call ours.

Your words have magic powers,
your energy healed my soul
you were the only woman who
could keep my heart whole.
I'm so desperate for your love, please hear my plea
I'm also terrified that you'll leave me.

I wake up in the morning, from a night of dreaming
realizing I'm alone as the sun starts gleaming.
The same feeling haunts my heart every day
until you visit my dream and my pain goes away.

OUR FAMILY

With your eyes bleak and your
face stricken with sadness
your tears fall on my shoulder, staining the plaid.
You endured suffering with such peaceful grace
in this game we call life, a rat race.

While you read, don't push the thoughts away
close your eyes and give yourself leeway.

Picture us together, filled with glee
watching as the songbirds sing in the trees.
We're sitting on my porch, in a lawn chair,
surrounding our loved ones, not a trace of despair.

Around the table in the backyard
is where our family plays cards
Scopa, pinochle, and gin rummy bets
and endless talk about Joe Namath of the Jets.

As the day winds down and the sun slowly sets
there had already been a few fights over lost bets.
The once blue sky slowly turns grey,
while a group of fireflies quietly light the way.

With our family, the party never stops
as we begin to judge the best belly flop.
The breeze soon came, and I
would change my clothes,
you follow me into the house and
say, "Shhh! nobody knows."

For the short time we disappear,
our family's focus will already veer.
We will play board games all night long
and that's when I will realize
that you're never wrong.

Finally asleep, dawn as dawn draws near
I will look at you and say, "I hope I was clear."
Every time we close our eyes and try to perceive
this could be real, you just have to believe.

I HATE YOU

I never thought I could say these words
but I feel it in my heart and bones when I see birds.
I feel intense love, one difficult for me to describe
I also feel hate and it's hard to characterize.

I ask myself, how could hate and love coexist
but it didn't take me long to get the gist
these are the ins and outs of a healthy relationship.
At least this long ride hasn't been a boring trip.

I guess what it is that I'm trying to say
I feel that you're slowly leaving me
and I'm begging you to stay.
Everything we once had is slowly going away
not our love, but our words, and our time to play.

I know this isn't what's supposed to be going on
but could you blame me? I dream
carelessly on the lawn.
It breaks my heart, every time I
see a bird leave its flock
footsteps dragging behind me on
the world's longest walk.

I find myself angry with you more than ever before
you push me away, like I'm some sort of a bore.
I know, of course, this isn't true
I want you to fight for me and say
please stay, because I love you.

No one did this for me, not my mom,
not my dad, and past lovers too.
Can't you understand, you're the
only love I ever knew?
I know you're trying to do the best by
me, and your intentions are true
but please I beg you, see it from my view.

Sometimes I can be a little much,
but the truth is, honestly, I just crave your touch
I want to feel your soft skin on mine
while you sing in my ear, with your voice so divine.

Screaming from the top of my lungs,
"Fight for me woman!"
Such passion rolling off my tongue
Yet in the same breath,
"I hate you! Shut up! Let's fight to the death!"

Sealing our quarrel with a long yearning lust
throwing you on the bed with one quick thrust
with a burning fire of passion in my eyes
I think we've both had enough of the good guy.

You'd be all mine, and nothing else would matter
I bet you'd rather do this than talk, enough chatter!
The gleaming shine of pleasure in your eyes
your body and mind are my true prize.

What it really is that I'm trying to say
is I'm angry you're taking yourself away.
You're all I have, in a world that's so blue
now the least you could do, is say, I love you.

A LOVE THAT LIGHTS THE WAY

We watched them grow
a life spent together, not as two, but one.
Dedication to those little lives we created
but now, it's our turn to dance in the sun.

A crash and boom, God creates life
a father smiles, a baby in the belly of his wife.
He lies down with his head against hers
in awe of creation and creator.

A mother, a lifeline, welcomes her baby to this earth
cuddled against her breast, her baby cries.
an everlasting love, between mother and child
becomes her purpose.

As our bodies tired, our baby grew,
the dancing light of the sun slowly faded.
A life filled with purpose and memories
of what we left behind.

THE LOSS OF MY POWER

There aren't enough words that can describe
how the love of a woman brought me to life.
A force that rivals only God,
ripping the power from my fingertips.

Filled with infinite wisdom of her Queen's past
a philosopher, with a gentle understanding of life.
Calming my mind, with her two hands
reminding me of the things I can't control.

Stricken with fear, my heart beat fast
there was little I could do to change the past.
Life is unpredictable and I'm forced to understand
we are at the mercy of God's hand.

There was little for me to concede,
I was convinced there was something I must need.
The power to control, and save those I love,
from the demons that walk this earth,
cast away from heaven above.

It was time for her to go, and I was left alone
the floors creaked, as I knelt and atoned.
I give my power to you, God,
for I am flawed.

ONE SECOND

One second, two, three, four,
hands ticked and foot tapped.
One day, two, three, four
there would soon be no time.

One second, two, three, four,
the sound of tears bounced off the tile floor.
One day, two, three, four,
a broken heart searched for fertile life.

One month, two, three, four,
he kissed her, watching the hands tick.
One second, two, three, four,
the news soon came, and her life changed.

TWO HEARTS

Two hearts bound by one soul
burning with the shine of the sun
and the glow of the moon
with the power to change the tides of destiny.

Two hearts linked by chain
on a rosary of everlasting love
never daring to say her name in vain
with the loyalty of a Mourning Dove.

Two hearts living in peace of mind
a hidden treasure that rivals gold
battling the fire that is mankind
with the grace of warrior angels.

Two hearts forever beating in sync
pumping the blood of life into our brains,
even when we don't think,
impenetrable, even by the cut of a diamond knife.

FOREVER

If we found your forever, what would it be?
The first thing that comes to mind is you and me.
I'd be your man, a knight in shining armor
or if you'd rather, a persimmon farmer.

I picture a house, with a white picket fence
a puppy, of course, would also make sense.
Two people coming from broken homes
starting from scratch, with a family of our own.

I do believe with all my heart
there will be days when you fart,
when a ferocious battle tears us apart
Only for us to make up, which is my favorite part.

I wouldn't be able to keep my hands off of you
no time for cuddling, there'd be too much to do.
How long would be enough? Maybe a day or two
believe it or not, that would only be a quick preview.

I guess what I'm trying to say,
is that even *forever* won't have perfect days.
Yes, that statement is very bold,
but I am sure, our love will never grow old.

I'd take care of you when you have the flu
enjoying every moment of growing old with you.
The time would age us, our hair would soon be grey
as we look back on the life we created one day.

As we grow old, there's a growing fear of living alone
the thing is, you're truly my one home.
You live in my heart, as the time passes by
the very thought of forever, brings a tear to my eye.

QUIRKY GIRL

Once a week, I passed her by on the street,
staring only at my feet.
I could feel her smile, like the breeze
during a summer night,
why couldn't I just ask her for a light?

I felt defeated, this woman was gone,
I had no leg left to stand on.
Then, there suddenly came a day,
when I saw this mystery girl on Broadway.

Spinning and dancing with the freedom
of a graceful bird,
it was impossible for her not to be heard.
Beaming with charisma, she stole the show,
it was then, I decided,
there was something I need to know.

I made my way backstage,
past the witch costumes and the smell of sage.
Next to the mirror, she powdered her nose,
still dressed in her quirky clothes.
Lo and behold,
my quirky girl was far from ice-cold,
she was so warm and bubbly
I decided to ask if she was a little hungry.

As the summer wind blew by
I asked my quirky girl to be my bride.
With tears in her eyes, she looked at me,
and said, "I'll always love you endlessly."

We shared a life, the years flew by
one day I looked at my quirky girl and cried
I always said, "I'll love you so."
But I'm afraid life dealt me the final blow.

Years later here I am,
sick and frail, a shell of a man.
My quirky girl held my hand
and said, "One day we'll both be
in the promised land."

I looked into my quirky girl's eyes one last time
and I couldn't find another rhyme.
I'll never forget that look on her face
when I handed her this poem, before it was too late.

For once, I was at a loss for words,
my quirky girl said, "You're being absurd."
She had felt our love from the very first day,
when I stared at my feet, without a word to say.

I look down on her every day
forever trying to keep my quirky
girl out of harm's way.
Until the day we meet again,
I'll see you in heaven, my best friend.

THE LOTTERY

I held four tickets in my hand,
a lottery winner, one lucky man.
Out of millions of people fate chose me,
it was clear these winnings were my destiny.

The signs of the universe guide me every day,
giving me this reward, free of taxes to pay.
The law, the man, can't take my money from me,
because my intentions are pure of heart,
and my mind is free.

My four tickets were useless,
my trump card was a pitch
it was never money that made men rich.
I have the love of a woman,
who was truly one in a million and three,
I mean, she's willing to spend
the rest of her life with me.

HOUSE OF CARDS

A smile hides the darkness within,
the dark side of the moon shows no light.
The demons, daring to arise
with total control over my mind.

The neurotransmitters unable to speak,
casting the darkness over the light.
A mere breath blew away the house of cards,
and my world fell apart.

In reality, everything was ok,
it was all a bad dream,
my loved ones begging me to stay.
I get lost in a world I create on my own,
never being able to get blood from a stone.

She tackled the bull by the horns,
not daring to ever break form.
Grounding me, as I create chaos in my life,
forgetting that this woman was *my* wife.

THE SIGNS OF THE UNIVERSE

Cardinals singing from the trees,
a person speaking Maltese,
the crash of the waves on the beach,
and even an empty car seat.

Tony Bennett crooning,
Frank Sinatra drinking,
Dean Martin swooning,
and Plato's thinking.

The singing church choir,
incessant compulsive shopping,
a deep sexual desire,
and unicorns frolicking.

The sizzle of a bloody steak,
vibrating piano strings,
homemade cheesecake,
and a blooming rose garden in spring.

There's a whole new world, and I opened my eyes
floating on the cloud called life
through transparent skies.
Heeding the signs of the universe and their cries,
signs from God, the Lord, my father, the wise.

THE DESERT OF LIFE

Foolishly challenging nature,
I pulled myself from the burning sand.
I'm not a coward, and I'd rather die a man,
I will not be afraid of a little heat and a golden tan.

The birds circled, awaiting the end of my quest,
it is the desert who is foolish to put
such a stubborn man to the test.
I will fight 'til my last breath,
to find my oasis, and defy my death.

Dying of thirst, trudging up the dune,
praying for the death of a star, the glow of the moon.
In awe of God, and his power over my life,
at the top was my thirst-quenching oasis—
a kiss from my wife.

PURE SUBSTANCE

The curdles appeared in my coffee cup
with an expiration date that didn't add up.
Such a putrid smell passed my nose,
a fate the universe clearly chose.

Sweet, creamy milk can turn sour,
even with the right temperature, gone by the hour.
It was in the cards for the milk to spoil,
like flowers refusing to sprout in barren soil.

I once had love that spoiled quicker than milk,
chunky and rotten, not creamy and smooth as silk.
True love won't spoil, like salt, sugar, and sulfur too,
Chemically unpredictable, yet
the same through and through.

HOME

The winds chased me, steering my ship,
the waves crashed, causing my boat to tip.
Shining a light from the mast,
trying to escape the storm of the past.

Like Odysseus before me, left for dead,
craving the sweet comfort of my bed.
With silk sheets and a warm body next to me,
surviving the storm to find Penelope.

Even Poseidon, God of the sea,
will not be able to stop me.
Ready for the waves and battles that wait,
because love is always stronger than hate.

MUSE

Never before did I bother to read,
or think I'd be enthralled by a Swede.
I was never a writer at heart I guess,
this was only the beginning of my blessing.

Stuck in a place where I feel so old,
I was never built to fit the world's mold.
It was you who always reminded me,
that myself was the best thing I could ever be.

I channeled my energy onto the page,
daring to tell the world of my story,
a life filled with rage.
Never did I dream I'd get to this stage,
I broke free of the shackles and fled my cage.

Our spirts will be forever intertwined,
you helped me open my eyes when I was blind.
A muse like you is impossible to find,
I thank God that I'm able to forever call you mine.

MOVIE MARATHON

Starting with *Godfather* one, two, and three,
you'll be forced to watch a movie marathon with me.
Generations of the world's greatest acts,
once I hit play, there's no going back.

I want you to watch when
Danny and Sandy first meet,
or when Dick Van Dyke invented toot sweets.
A long time ago in a galaxy far, far, away,
I bet you'll have a headache by the end of the day.

Rocky goes the distance and calls Adrian's name,
leaving out Willy Wonka would just be a shame.
As a child, I wanted to be just like Indiana Jones,
traveling the world, searching for ancient stones.

Borat will definitely lighten the mood,
I'm sure you'll enjoy watching Harry and Sally feud.
I bet you're hungry, let's go to Katz!
You'll have what's she's having, and that's that.

MUSIC LESSONS

My fingers grip the nylon strings,
feeling the joy that music brings.
Such sweet sounds, passing my ear,
the freedom of expression, world without fear.

Music is one of many ways for the soul to speak,
not meant for the faint of heart, those who are weak.
It takes a courageous person
to say how they truly feel,
revealing your dreams, a fate that appears sealed.

These dreams are not just in my head or heart,
the journey finding them out
will be my favorite part.
When you follow your bliss,
your life's dreams come true,
including finding a person that loves *you* for *you*.

EXPLORING THE WORLD

The bright shine of the Italian sun,
in the city of Firenze,
where the Renaissance had begun.
A house in the country,
of the land we call Pennsylvania,
spotting Dracula in the darkness of Transylvania.

The magnificent art of Vincent Van Gogh,
French wine in hand, with cheese and sourdough.
Riding a gondola through the Venetian canals,
sharing pretzels with our German pals.

The rush and excitement of New York City,
singing along to *West Side Story*, "I feel pretty!"
Laying on the golden sand of Mykonos, Greece,
captivated by the beauty of Versailles,
where the Allies made peace.

Our trip would finish with great Paella from Spain,
as we danced the fandango in the rain.
Such passion in our bodies and love in our hearts,
a lesson of culture, from a world filled with art.

WHEN I DIE

When I die, I want to be burned,
coming from a life where I have learned
all the beauty of God's creation,
happy with life's duration.

When I die, I want to make peace,
with those I hate and those I love.
To forgive and heal the scars of the past,
my world tranquil, at last.

When I die, please respect me,
spread my ashes under a shady tree,
near a blooming rose garden too,
so my soul could finally be free.

When I die, make sure I'm near
the woman I swore to protect and nurture,
even in death, my spirit will shroud her,
where it's impossible to predict what will occur.

JUST BREATHE

I never realized I was blind,
when I found myself in this bind.
Terrified of the unknown,
as I stare away in comfort at my phone.

It's easy to hide from life around you,
those without scars are far and few.
Suffering alone, because there's no one left to ask
about your future, about God's next task.

Why have faith you say?
The answer is, I simply prayed,
asking God to show me a sign,
he told me the power was mine.

The love of another forces you to grow,
I became a better man, scaring away the evil crow.
The terrifying feeling inside of me
disappeared, when all I did was breathe.

SHE WROTE TO ME

She wrote to me, about her shoes,
and how easily she bruised.
Carefully drawing me in,
with a silent smile, a seductive grin.

She wrote to me, using her eyes,
as I saw the pain, when she cried.
The feeling of longing on her face,
praying to live out her days in a magical place.

She wrote to me about her life,
how the thought of the past pierced
her heart with a knife,
and how the future scared her so,
longing for my care with a childlike glow.

She wrote to me about things I couldn't understand,
a country mouse, who never had anything planned.
Living like a princess, in a bubble of her own,
teaching me about true love,
something I had never known.

MAKING SAUCE

A recipe deeply guarded,
starting with freshly chopped garlic.
Imported extra virgin olive oil,
salting the water when it comes to a boil.

Canned tomatoes? I beg your pardon?
I'll get them fresh from my garden!
Tony Bennett, playing in the background,
get the fresh pasta, about a pound.

Don't forget to stir the sauce!
I didn't mean to yell, I know you're the boss.
Giving her the power, I decided to be smart,
"I'll set the table, sweetheart."

We sat down ready for a great meal,
as I waited for her to make a big deal.
It didn't take long for her to admit,
my sauce is the best, fuhgeddaboudit!

LUNCHTIME

Life finally threw me a bone,
a moment I believe I created on my own.
When you see something so vividly in your mind,
it will eventually reveal itself in time.

God locked a door and rolled the dice,
it was time for me to listen to my own advice.
When you're a good person, life truly rewards you,
giving the love of a lifetime its debut.

The chance to realize all my dreams were true,
and that dreams could never justify being with you.
A lifetime passed by only lunchtime,
asking me to buy you food was never a crime.

ABOUT THE AUTHOR

PHOTO BY SOFIA MONGE

ANTHONY SCIARRATTA was born in Maspeth, New York, to Italian-American parents. He holds a Bachelor of Arts in Media Studies from Queens College and a Master of Arts in Communications from the New York Institute of Technology. Anthony takes great pride in labeling himself an old soul. His love for classic films, music, and literature shows through his work. *Faith in the Unknown* is Anthony's debut book of poetry.